W9-COW-592

Don't miss this!

Social Media

Connect with a community of *Bible Studies for Life* users. Post responses to questions, share teaching ideas, and link to great blog content.
Facebook.com/BibleStudiesForLife

Get instant updates about new articles, giveaways, and more. **@BibleMeetsLife**

The App

Simple and straightforward, this elegantly designed iPhone app gives you all the content of the Group Member Book—plus a whole lot more—right at your fingertips. Available in the iTunes App Store; search **"Bible Studies for Life."**

Blog

At **BibleStudiesForLife.com/blog** you will find magazine articles and music downloads from LifeWay Worship. Plus, leaders and group members alike will benefit from the blog posts written for people in every life stage—singles, parents, boomers, and senior adults—as well as media clips, connections between our study topics, current events, and much more.

Pressure Points
Bible Studies for Life: Small Group Member Book

© 2013 LifeWay Press®

ISBN: 9781415875186

Item: 005600173

Dewey Decimal Classification Number: 155.9

Subject Heading: STRESS MANAGEMENT \ CHRISTIAN LIFE \ BIBLE. N.T. JAMES--STUDY

Eric Geiger
Vice President, Church Resources

Ronnie Floyd
General Editor

David Francis
Managing Editor

Brian Gass
Karen Dockrey
Content Editors

Philip Nation
Director, Adult Ministry Publishing

Faith Whatley
Director, Adult Ministry

Send questions/comments to: Content Editor, *Bible Studies for Life: Adults*, One LifeWay Plaza, Nashville, TN 37234-0175; or make comments on the Web at *www.BibleStudiesforLife.com*

Printed in the United States of America

For ordering or inquiries, visit *www.lifeway.com*; write LifeWay Small Groups; One LifeWay Plaza; Nashville, TN 37234-0152; or call toll free (800) 458-2772.

HCSB—All Scripture quotations, unless otherwise indicated, are taken from the Holman Christian Standard Bible®, copyright 1999, 2000, 2002, 2003, 2009 by Holman Bible Publishers. Used by permission.

Bible Studies for Life: Adults often lists websites that may be helpful to our readers. Our staff verifies each site's usefulness and appropriateness prior to publication. However, website content changes quickly so we encourage you to approach all websites with caution. Make sure sites are still appropriate before sharing them with students, friends, and family.

Pressure. It's everywhere.

Coaches and players are under pressure: "Win or else!"

Business leaders face the pressure to make a profit.

Teenagers feel the pressure to follow their peers.

Couples endure the pressure of raising children, balancing budgets, and trying to hold their marriages together.

Doctors prescribe medication like never before to help stressed people deal with the pressure of life.

Pressure is nothing new. James, the half brother of Jesus, wrote to Jewish Christians in the first century who faced intense pressure. They had been dispersed because of persecution, and they faced increasing pressure to let faith live only in their heads instead of being lived out in their lives. They faced the pressure to wilt in times of trial and the pressure to compromise when facing temptation. They faced the pressure to cave in to prejudicial preference when welcoming people into their gatherings and to let their tongues wag out of control. They faced the pressure to demand their own way and the pressure to retaliate when mistreated.

James beckoned these first believers to let the pressure push them deeper in their journey with Jesus. And James invites you to open your life to the truth of God's Word and learn how to deal positively with the pressure points of life. Pressure doesn't have to dismantle your faith. Let pressure lead you to experience the presence and power of God like never before.

Chip Henderson

The six-week study "Pressure Points" was developed and written by Dr. Chip Henderson, Senior Pastor at Pinelake Church in Brandon, Mississippi. Chip is a graduate of New Orleans Baptist Theological Seminary, and has been married for 21 years to Christy. They have three children. He is an avid hunter, runner, and triathlete. Chip is the co-creator of the *L3 Journal* and the author of the young adult study *Samson: A Life Well Wasted* (LifeWay).

Chip's hope is that as you engage in this study, you will avoid the pressures that mess up our lives.

SESSION 1

THE PRESSURE OF TRIALS

contents

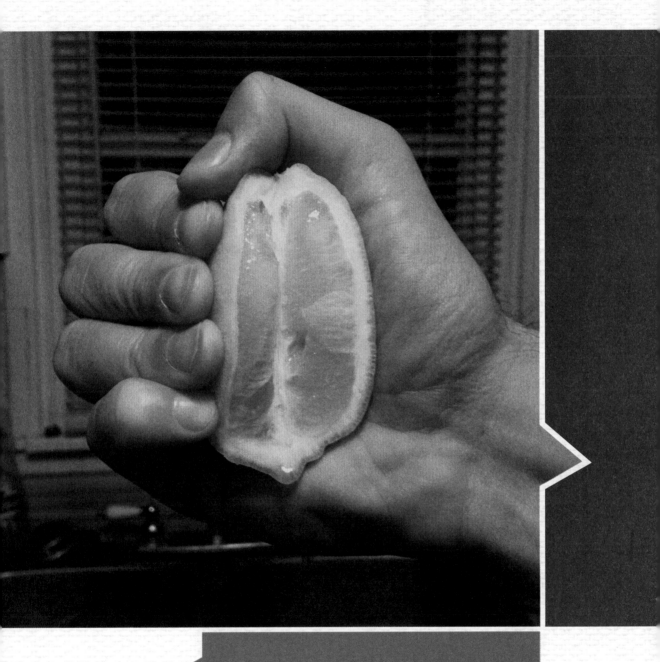

What pressures squeeze the joy out of life?

Joyful trust in God will see you through all trials.

THE BIBLE MEETS LIFE

No one lives a problem-free life.

My mom used to say when life gives you a lemon, just make lemonade. But that's a whole lot easier said than done. I got a call from a friend whose wife was told she has cancer. I have a friend who has been married less than a year and his wife just announced to him that she's leaving. I talked to a young dad who is devastated that he is losing his job. Meanwhile, his wife is expecting a child in a couple of months. Where's the lemonade amidst those lemons?

The Bible is full of people who were dealt hard hands, but through faith in God and through perseverance, they made sweet lemonade: Joseph, Moses, Ruth, Hannah, David, etc. The list is long. But each found triumph through God, amidst the messes. They moved from victims to victors. In James 1 we have a game plan for overcoming trials and finding joy, even amidst those terribly unfair trials.

WHAT DOES THE BIBLE SAY?

James 1:1-4 *(HCSB)*

1 James, a slave of God and of the Lord Jesus Christ:
To the 12 tribes in the Dispersion. Greetings.

2 Consider it a great joy, my brothers, whenever you
experience various trials,

3 knowing that the testing of your faith produces
endurance.

4 But endurance must do its complete work, so that
you may be mature and complete, lacking nothing.

Key Words

slave (v. 1) – This humble title signifies ownership by, absolute obligation to, and readiness to obey a master.

trials (v. 2) – Trials are difficulties and afflictions that can strengthen our faith and prove its genuineness as in 1 Peter 1:6-7.

mature and complete (v. 4) – Mature may refer to relative maturity as compared with immaturity (Eph. 4:13) or to final perfection in the coming age (1 Cor. 13:10). Complete refers to entire or whole, with no unsoundness whatsoever.

James 1:1-2

Two problems with encountering trials are you don't expect them, and they surround you. You may fall into an unforeseen situation. You may lose your health and/or wealth (Luke 10:30; Acts 27:41). James tells us trials are inevitable: it's not *if* you encounter them, but *when* you encounter them.

Trials are varied. They come in all shapes and sizes:

▶ **Temptation** – An enticement to sin, whether it's a click on a website, a cruel word, or a hatred harbored.

▶ **Sickness** – Sometimes its not your sickness, but the sickness of another person.

▶ **Persecution** – Even Jesus Christ suffered; so suffering for Jesus is to be expected for believers.

▶ **Trouble** – It could be any adversity, affliction, or circumstances sent by God—or allowed by Him—to test or prove your faith, holiness or character. Such troubles can be financial hardship, bad news, difficult people, hard circumstances, troubled relationships, broken cars, or layoffs.

The reference to joy is actually the first phrase in verse 2. Joy may not be your first attitude. When you run aground or fall into a pit, your instinct is to feel hurt, startled, mad, and reactionary. Joy may not be your initial reaction, but it is a choice you make through the power of God. Through God, joy becomes your ultimate attitude.

What keeps you from reacting with joy when the pressure of life feels overwhelming?

QUESTION #1

How does joy become your ultimate attitude? Consider it so.

"Consider" comes from a root that means to lead, to bring, or to carry. It is the concept of evaluating, and then based on the evaluation, leading your mind, attitude, and actions in God's direction. "Consider it a great joy" is an imperative, which means it is a command. Joy is a careful and deliberate decision.

Don't rely on feelings. Give due consideration to what God asks you to do about what has happened. Let Him show you the facts. Let Him manage your feelings. Listen for what He's telling you to do. Then do it.

> **What emotions did you feel during your most recent trial?**

QUESTION #2

HERE COMES THE TRIAL:

A loved one has been diagnosed with a serious illness.

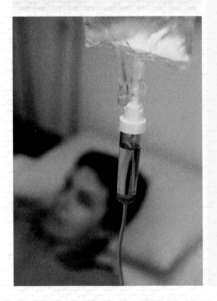

1. Joy and trust in God could benefit me by:

....

....

....

2. Joy and trust in God could benefit this loved one by:

....

....

....

3. Joy and trust in God could benefit others by:

....

....

....

James 1:3

Faith is a muscle that must be exercised to gain strength. The less you use faith, the easier it is to lose it. One of the times we need those faith muscles most is during trials. It's easier to be patient with my spouse when I'm in a cheerful mood. But what if I'm pressed and grouchy? Then I watch God accomplish something very specific: patience and kindness that endure.

Endurance is one of God's goals in tests. He develops staying power in believers. Endurance means to be unswerving from God's purposes. We show our loyalty to Him amidst the trials and amidst the joys. Yes, we're sad about the trial. Yes, we're so weary we can scarcely put one foot in front of the other. But God produces endurance in His people. We sometimes call that perseverance, faithfulness, or steadfastness. It is God's work of developing our spiritual muscle and resolve to stand firm.

How do I consider it joy in the middle of a trial? By knowing what God will do. Trials aren't a test of your personal strength or wisdom; they test your faith in God to see you through. God Himself is with you. He is developing staying power in you.

Remember the story Jesus told about the soils (Luke 8:4-15)? Many people hear the word, but in the end, the only seed that was fruitful was the seed that *endured* in the soil. If you are ever going to bear fruit in your Christian life, then perseverance and staying power are not optional. If you are being tested it means:

▶ You are a child of God so you have faith.

▶ You have a faith worth developing and refining.

▶ God will strengthen and prepare you.

▶ You have the assurance of the presence of God.

> *During your most recent trial, how did you see God walking with you?*
>
> QUESTION #3

> "If we live only for the present and forget the future, then trials will make us bitter, not better"

— WARREN W. WIERSBE

How have you been encouraged by the endurance of others during trials?

QUESTION #4

James 1:4

Endurance takes time. Endurance takes day-after-day action. Endurance must be guided by God. Otherwise it won't do it's job—it will be incomplete. It will lack. I must consent to let endurance shape and mold me until I am complete. When I submit to the process of endurance and allow the shaping and strengthening of my faith, the goal is ultimately reached: completeness, perfection, lacking nothing.

I can resist the work of endurance in my life and fight against it. I can run from it in favor of a trial-free life. I don't have to study; I can avoid that pain but then I won't pass, and that will bring pain of its own. I don't have to lift weights in the off season, but I don't have to win either. I don't have to let God complete me, but I'd miss out on all of my purposes in life. Which is less painful? Both paths can be painful, but one brings about pointless pain and wasted grief. The pain endured through trials is both positive and progressive, moving you toward a happy and rewarding end.

God is working around your life so that He can also work in and through your life. He guides you to be 100 percent complete in Him. Embrace His work; become open, pliable, humble, and teachable.

▶ **Perfect** – Having reached its end; complete, mature, fully developed.

▶ **Complete** – Fully developed; running at full capacity with nothing unused.

▶ **Lacking Nothing** – Nothing left out or left behind. You are fully equipped and prepared.

LIVE IT OUT

So what does God want you to do when trials come your way?

▶ **Choose a joyful attitude.** Evaluate how a joy-filled attitude could alleviate the pressure you feel from life.

▶ **Share your story.** Explain to someone how, during a previous trial, God strengthened you through the difficult time.

▶ **Help someone who is struggling**. Find someone who is going through difficulty. Be available to listen, encourage, and help them.

God is working in you. He is working in every circumstance, both good and bad to bring about the development of His character and power in you so that you may be perfect, complete, and useful for His glory. Despite life's circumstances, God gives us the capability to turn sour into sweet. ***Now go make lemonade.***

Weathering the Storms of Life

A highway sign on Wyoming's South Pass flashed a warning: INCLEMENT WEATHER. NO UNNECESSARY TRAVEL. My husband, Shane, drove while our 6-month-old, Ellie, and I were nestled peacefully in the backseat. It seemed implausible to me that on a quiet spring day, a sudden snowstorm could besiege a stretch of that sunny mountain pass. Shane's words assured me, "It will be all right." But those five words were his last. In an instant, I was stripped of all that I treasured: my beloved spouse, my delightful baby girl, my health, my financial security, and my ministry.

To continue reading "Weathering the Storms of Life" from *HomeLife* magazine, visit *BibleStudiesforLife.com/articles*.

My group's prayer requests

....

....

....

....

....

....

....

....

....

....

My thoughts

SESSION 2

THE PRESSURE OF TEMPTATION

What food tempts you to say yes to just one more bite?

God won't tempt me, but He will provide a way to resist temptation.

THE BIBLE MEETS LIFE

Just one more slice—one more bite—there's no harm in that, right?

Satan wants you to believe it's OK to give in to temptation. Who'll know? Where's the harm? Give in to the little temptations and you'll find yourself giving in to the big ones. We all know someone who lied and lost their reputation, the flirtatious person at the office who lost their marriage, or someone who gave in to the temptation of gossip only to lose their best friend. Temptations promise good things, but in the end they always fail to deliver. The Bible is full of people who gave in to temptation and lost it all, but it also contains stories of men and women who successfully resisted temptation. What did they know that we don't?

God doesn't tempt us. Instead He provides a way for us to resist temptation and escape its harm.

So what's it going to be? One more bite, or will you put the fork down? James 1:13-18 has the plan of action for resisting temptation and living in a way that pleases Christ.

WHAT DOES THE BIBLE SAY?

James 1:13-18 (HCSB)

13 No one undergoing a trial should say, "I am being tempted by God." For God is not tempted by evil, and He Himself doesn't tempt anyone.

14 But each person is tempted when he is drawn away and enticed by his own evil desires.

15 Then after desire has conceived, it gives birth to sin, and when sin is fully grown, it gives birth to death.

16 Don't be deceived, my dearly loved brothers.

17 Every generous act and every perfect gift is from above, coming down from the Father of lights; with Him there is no variation or shadow cast by turning.

18 By His own choice, He gave us a new birth by the message of truth so that we would be the firstfruits of His creatures.

Key Words

trial/tempt (vv. 13-14) – These words come from the same Greek word. Context determines whether the word is used for trials (referring to difficulties and hardships as in verse 2) or enticements to sin.

evil desires (v. 14) – The single Greek word means a longing or desire. It can be a good or natural desire, but it is usually used to refer to something forbidden.

James 1:13

James wrote to Christians who, like us, faced the pressures of temptation. He outlined the truth about temptation and showed how to handle it. In the previous session we studied about trials, but temptations are different. Trials bring the pressure of hardship or difficulty. There is nothing necessarily good or pleasurable about a trial. Job lost everything (Job 1–2). Abraham was asked to sacrifice his son Isaac (Gen. 22). There was no appeal in those.

But there is appeal in temptation. The pressure comes through its appeal. The appeal of temptation is typically characterized by promises:

> ▶ **Temptation promises you some gain.** The gain may be fun, money, pleasure, adventure, position, or an appeased palate. The grass of temptation will always appear green.

> ▶ **Temptation promises you won't get hurt**. You can get away with it. Nobody will know. It's not even that wrong. You won't get burned like others. You are different. You can handle it.

Being tempted isn't wrong, but giving in is. Temptation promises that you will be better off after you indulge, but you won't. James communicates two truths:

> ▶ **Temptation is inevitable but not irresistible**. It's not a matter of *if* you are tempted, but *when* you are tempted. Temptation comes to all of us. It even came to Jesus (Matt. 4:1-11). Temptation comes to a pastor as surely as it comes to any member of his church.

> ▶ **Temptation never comes from God**. We know this because of what God has revealed in His Word. We know this because of God's nature. He is untemptable. He lacks nothing and needs nothing. No evil offer appeals to God. He does not tempt us because He is good, loving, and righteous. He cannot and will not pressure us to do anything contrary to His character.

> *If temptations promise good but never deliver, why do we so often say yes to them?*
>
> **QUESTION #1**

QUESTION #2

In what ways are we tempted to satisfy a God-given desire in a sinful way?

"God is faithful, and He will not allow you to be tempted beyond what you are able, but with the temptation He will also provide a way of escape"

—1 CORINTHIANS 10:13

James 1:14-15

Temptation is unique for every person. Temptation comes when each of us is carried off by our own desires. The Greek word for "own" is *idios*. "Idiosyncrasy" comes from it. It's unique to you. Therefore, what may tempt me may not tempt you. Some are easily tempted to react in anger to a situation; others seldom get angry. Some are tempted by sexual opportunities; others stay away. Some are tempted to engage in gluttony or other excess; others walk away from another helping. You face some temptations that others around you don't. But they face temptations you don't face.

Temptation follows a predictable process. The process in James 1:14-15 can be illustrated with fishing. An angler throws bait to an unsuspecting bass. When a worm dangles before him, his desire wakens. He swims away from the safety of his log and swallows the bait. The fish is no longer in control. He is pulled against his will toward the angler's boat, net, cooler, and maybe the taxidermist. What bait is used on us? James says we are tempted when we get carried away and enticed. We have desires—maybe even God-given desires—for food, sex, approval, shelter, love, or power. These aren't bad in themselves, but fulfilling them in wrong ways is deadly (Mark 4:19, Col. 3:5, 1 Tim. 6:9). When we leave the safety and shelter of God's provision we take Satan's bait. Sin conceives in us. Sin entangles. We suffer.

James 1:16-18

So how do we deal with the pressure of temptation? We draw upon the good and perfect gifts God gives to us. Instead of leading us to evil, God provides what we need to live righteously, and resist temptation:

▶ **A relationship with Christ**—Too many of us think we are helpless to resist temptation. But as a child of God, the power of Christ in you gives you victory over sin. As a Christian—a saint—you are called to be holy and blameless. Because you are a child of God, you can successfully resist temptation. Jesus Christ takes up residence in your life and empowers you by His Holy Spirit. So repent, and call on God's power to live like a Christ-follower.

▶ **God's Word**—When Jesus was tempted, He used Scripture to respond to the pressure of temptation (Matt. 4:4). Since Jesus, who is God, used Scripture to resist temptation, how much more should we? What better way to overcome the pressure of temptation than repeating and obeying the Word of the One who made us and who knows us better than we know ourselves? When we memorize God's Word and hide it in our hearts, we have the ability to give the right answer at the right time. God's Word becomes our defense (Ps. 119:11).

▶ **An escape route**—One of God's greatest gifts to us is the promise from 1 Corinthians 10:13. God will provide a way of escape and help us stand up to any temptation we face. God the creator and sustainer of the universe, the One who knows everything and everyone, promises to provide us with the ability to resist the pressure of temptation. God's escape route may be a telephone ringing, a whisper in your conscience, or a friend keeping you accountable. But God does not stop us without our participation.

Yes, we need to call out to the Spirit of Christ inside of us for help. Yet we also need to not walk past God's opportunity to bail out. We can also escape by avoiding those things that lead us toward temptation and by doing those things that make us stronger, more like God. The pressure of temptation is great—but God is greater and He has provided us with all that we need to resist that pressure.

> *What are some other gifts God has provided that could help you resist temptation?*

QUESTION #3

How can you support and encourage someone struggling with temptation?

QUESTION **#4**

Choose one of these circumstances and identify a way of escape:

THE **CIRCUMSTANCE**	THE **ESCAPE**
1. I'm lonely and in a hotel room with Wi-Fi and cable:	
2. The cashier gave me too much cash back:	
3. An "exaggeration" on my application will help me land this job:	

LIVE IT OUT

Being tempted isn't wrong. But the longer we consider a temptation, the weaker we get. So choose God's way of escape:

▶ **Think about the temptations you face.** Pray, asking God to help you recognize and do His strategy to overcome each.

▶ **Memorize Proverbs 4:25.** Practice it in moments of temptation.

▶ **Find a friend you can trust.** Ask him or her to hold you accountable as you face temptation.

Sin may offer temporary pleasure, but we will experience consequences when we give in to temptation. Put down the fork. **Choose God's way of escape.**

A Marriage Redeemed

Magical. It's really the only word that described the week our family had just spent. It was a once-in-a-lifetime trip—the kind you dream, plan, and save for—it had been a fairy tale.

We were on the long drive home to Texas, the kids asleep in the back of our van. I was tired, too, but on a high that comes from making dreams come true. I didn't know my "perfect world" was about to end.

To continue reading "A Marriage Redeemed" from *HomeLife* magazine, visit *BibleStudiesforLife.com/articles*.

My group's prayer requests

....

....

....

....

....

....

....

....

....

....

My thoughts

SESSION 3

THE PRESSURE OF PARTIALITY

Who or what does society value most?

God does not play favorites and neither should I.

THE BIBLE MEETS LIFE

A church made national news recently when they made a couple find a new place to get married on the day before their wedding. The reason? They were the "wrong" race. A few in the church pressured the pastor. He could do the wedding in their church building and get fired, or he could move the wedding and keep his job. He caved.

Discrimination too often raises its ugly head. Christians in the early church also felt pressure to give preferential treatment to certain folks based on their economic standing.

Discrimination has no place in church or anywhere in our lives. Why? The ground at the foot of the cross is level. God makes no distinction between Jew and Greek, slave and free, male and female, rich and poor, one race and another race, Democrat or Republican. God plays no favorites and neither should we.

The invitation of Jesus is "whosoever will may come." Let's consider some principles from James that will equip us to refuse the pressure of favoritism.

WHAT DOES THE BIBLE SAY?

James 2:1-13 *(HCSB)*

1 My brothers, do not show favoritism as you hold on to the faith in our glorious Lord Jesus Christ.

2 For example, a man comes into your meeting wearing a gold ring and dressed in fine clothes, and a poor man dressed in dirty clothes also comes in.

3 If you look with favor on the man wearing the fine clothes and say, "Sit here in a good place," and yet you say to the poor man, "Stand over there," or, "Sit here on the floor by my footstool,"

4 haven't you discriminated among yourselves and become judges with evil thoughts?

5 Listen, my dear brothers: Didn't God choose the poor in this world to be rich in faith and heirs of the kingdom that He has promised to those who love Him?

6 Yet you dishonored that poor man. Don't the rich oppress you and drag you into the courts?

7 Don't they blaspheme the noble name that was pronounced over you at your baptism?

8 Indeed, if you keep the royal law prescribed in the Scripture, Love your neighbor as yourself, you are doing well.

9 But if you show favoritism, you commit sin and are convicted by the law as transgressors.

10 For whoever keeps the entire law, yet fails in one point, is guilty of breaking it all.

11 For He who said, Do not commit adultery, also said, Do not murder. So if you do not commit adultery, but you do murder, you are a lawbreaker.

12 Speak and act as those who will be judged by the law of freedom.

13 For judgment is without mercy to the one who hasn't shown mercy. Mercy triumphs over judgment.

Key Words

favoritism (v. 1) – This literally means receiving or lifting the face. Ancient subjects would prostrate themselves to seek a ruler's favor. If he lifted their faces, they would be heard. The word came to mean showing favor on improper grounds, often social or political.

James 2:1-4

We say, "Don't judge a book by it's cover." But that's exactly what Christians in the first century were guilty of doing. They made judgments based on outward appearance and first impressions. Specifically, they showed preference to the wealthy over the poor.

James asked that if a well-dressed man comes to your meeting wearing fine clothes and plenty of "bling," do you pay special attention to him? Do you give preferential treatment? If a homeless person stumbles in, do you relegate him to a section in the back? The answer in the first century was, "Yes!" How different are we?

▶ If the house next door is for sale and a family of a different ethnicity takes a tour, do you secretly hope they don't buy?

▶ If two people walk into your business, one in overalls and the other in business casual attire, who do you help more willingly?

▶ If a person with money shows up at your church, do you take special measures to make sure he or she has a good experience?

The ugly truth is we prefer people who look like us, act like us, and serve our needs or meet our standards. We don't like "their kind"— whatever that means.

God doesn't discriminate (Acts 10:34; 15:9, Gal. 3:28), so why do we?

When we show favoritism, we become judges with evil thoughts. God wants us to make wise judgments about people (Matt. 10:16). But when our judgments have selfish and evil motives—picking people who can help us, or rejecting those we don't like, or discrediting those we don't understand—then we miss God's heart.

> ***What kinds of experiences affect who we want to be around?***
>
> QUESTION #1

James 2:5-7

The outer trappings just can't tell what's inside. For example, wealth does not make someone more powerful or rich. James says God actually chose the poor of this world to be rich in things that matter. Christianity has always had a special place for the poor (Luke 4:18; 1 Cor. 1:26). In James 1:26-27, James says true religion expresses God's heart. It looks after widows and orphans—the poorest of the poor. Even so, being poor isn't more holy than having resources. James 1:26-27 doesn't say God shuts the door on the rich. The Bible doesn't condemn people who work hard and earn good money.

▶ **The problem was not money, but how people in the church treated people with money.** The church was making rich people feel welcomed and poor people feel shunned. This dishonors the poor person who is also resourceful and who is also made in the image of God.

▶ **Another problem was the way some rich people were behaving.** Deferring to the rich may not end up well for you. The rich are not always as pure as the wind-driven snow. James says these rich people were guilty of oppressing the Christians and dragging them into court. Some blasphemed Jesus.

Several years ago the governor of Kentucky wanted to attend a particular church on a Sunday morning. He had his people call the church to let them know he would attend and to ask where the governor should park and sit. To their credit, this church informed the governor that he was free to park wherever he wanted to and sit anywhere there was an open seat, but nothing would be reserved. You may say that was disrespectful, but they believed it was being impartial. The governor gets no more special treatment than a middle school football coach. When we show partiality, we miss the heart of God.

> *Why is the heart of God so close to those who are poor and excluded?*

QUESTION #2

"Prejudice is a great time saver. You can form opinions without having to get the facts."

E. B. WHITE

James 2:8-13

Jesus said the whole Law is summed up in this: love God and love others as ourselves (one place he said this is Matt. 22:37-40). You are doing well if you are fulfilling that law. Showing love pleases God.

But notice what James says is true if you show partiality: it means you make a judgment based on the outside or the face value of a person. When the way you treat people changes based on the attractiveness of their appearance, the color of their skin, the cars they drive, or any other false measure, then you are guilty of favoritism. You are committing sin.

We tend to minimize favoritism or harbor racism as if it's not so bad. At least we aren't murderers, we claim. But God doesn't grade on a curve. He doesn't say the "good sinners" will be OK. Sin is sin and the wages of sin is death whether you commit recognized sins or socially acceptable ones (Rom. 6:23).

FAVOR A DIFFERENT APPROACH

When in a conversation I hear a phrase like "those people" or "they're not like me," I will ...

....

When ridiculing jokes are told, I will ...

....

When I see someone treating another person as expendable, I will ...

....

What are examples of showing honor versus playing favorites?

QUESTION #3

As Christians, we are saved by God's grace through faith alone (Eph. 2:8-9). Thankfully, God empowers us to become the loving, merciful people He has called us to be:

▶ **By the power of the Holy Spirit dwelling within us, God will enable us to live the character of Christ.** The Spirit, through James, urges us to throw off favoritism and put on mercy toward all people. This happens as we obey God in the way we treat people.

▶ **We who have received Christ have been shown mercy; consequently we are to speak and act (v. 12) with mercy toward others.** Failing to show mercy calls into question a person's repentance of sin and experience of God's mercy. James' sobering statement in verse 13 is that the full judgment of God, "without mercy," will fall on such a person— "the one who hasn't shown mercy." But thanks be to God, His "mercy triumphs over judgment" for all who speak and act with love toward God and people.

> *What's at stake when I play favorites?*
>
> QUESTION #4

So here's the deal. If you treat people without mercy, you will be judged by that same standard. But if you show mercy, God will turn that mercy back to you. You reap what you sow.

LIVE IT OUT

If you have caved to the pressure of favoritism, make it right. Build a reputation for loving like God loves.

▶ **Check your attitude.** When you treat someone with partiality, check the attitude of your heart. Confess it to God.

▶ **Demonstrate God's love in action.** Deliberately say a kind word, welcome someone to your table, or build someone up. Go out of your way to care.

▶ **Build a friendship.** Spend time with someone you wouldn't typically relate to.

The pastor of the church who moved the wedding regretted his decision. He worked to make it right. No matter what happens around you, refuse to play favorites. **Value what God values and love indiscriminately.**

Hand in Hand

In his song "My Own Little World," artist Matthew West swallows hard about living where he never feels material want. There the population consists entirely of "me." Many of us have felt this same angst. Volunteers from Durham, N.C. are doing something about it.

To continue reading "Hand in Hand" from *More Living* magazine, visit *BibleStudiesforLife.com/articles*.

My group's prayer requests

....

....

....

....

....

....

....

....

....

....

My thoughts

SESSION 4

THE PRESSURE OF WORDS

When does your mouth get you into trouble?

Fuel your words with wisdom and gentleness.

THE BIBLE MEETS LIFE

Our culture lives in two extremes. At one end is political correctness. At the other is saying whatever you want in whatever way you want. The person who can use words wisely is the person who has found biblical balance. We do that by controlling our tongues.

Without the tongue, this two-ounce part of our anatomy, a mother couldn't sing her baby to sleep. Ambassadors would struggle to represent nations. Voices couldn't stretch the minds of students.

But our tongues act inconsistently. One person blesses the meal and then gossips while eating. A coach leads the Lord's Prayer to launch the game and then curses at his players. On the way to church a dad scolds and complains; then walks in to sing to God. Tongues aren't just inconsistent; they're deadly. They can produce verbal cyanide. Some words are lethal, relentless, and destructive. Words spoken carelessly, unwisely, and hastily can set ablaze family, church, and community. Words can kill.

WHAT DOES THE BIBLE SAY?

James 3:1-18 (HCSB)

1 Not many should become teachers, my brothers, knowing that we will receive a stricter judgment, 2 for we all stumble in many ways. If anyone does not stumble in what he says, he is a mature man who is also able to control his whole body. 3 Now when we put bits into the mouths of horses to make them obey us, we also guide the whole animal. 4 And consider ships: Though very large and driven by fierce winds, they are guided by a very small rudder wherever the will of the pilot directs. 5 So too, though the tongue is a small part of the body, it boasts great things. Consider how large a forest a small fire ignites. 6 And the tongue is a fire. The tongue, a world of unrighteousness, is placed among the parts of our bodies. It pollutes the whole body, sets the course of life on fire, and is set on fire by hell. 7 Every sea creature, reptile, bird, or animal is tamed and has been tamed by man, 8 but no man can tame the tongue. It is a restless evil, full of deadly poison.

9 We praise our Lord and Father with it, and we curse men who are made in God's likeness with it. 10 Praising and cursing come out of the same mouth. My brothers, these things should not be this way. 11 Does a spring pour out sweet and bitter water from the same opening? 12 Can a fig tree produce olives, my brothers, or a grapevine produce figs? Neither can a saltwater spring yield fresh water.

13 Who is wise and has understanding among you? He should show his works by good conduct with wisdom's gentleness. 14 But if you have bitter envy and selfish ambition in your heart, don't brag and deny the truth. 15 Such wisdom does not come from above but is earthly, unspiritual, demonic. 16 For where envy and selfish ambition exist, there is disorder and every kind of evil. 17 But the wisdom from above is first pure, then peace-loving, gentle, compliant, full of mercy and good fruits, without favoritism and hypocrisy. 18 And the fruit of righteousness is sown in peace by those who cultivate peace.

Key Words

a world of unrighteousness (v. 6) – Uncontrolled words activate all the world's wickedness.

a restless evil (v. 8) – Restless is translated "unstable" in v. 8. The tongue is treacherous, inconsistent, and uninhibited, always looking for trouble and creating mischief.

Praising and cursing (v. 10) – The tongue can heal or wound.

James 3:1-8

Destructive words come in all forms: profane words, hateful words, angry words, thoughtless words, mean words, selfish words, critical words, sarcastic words, and dishonest words. Some people deliver destructive words through yelling and screaming. Others inject the same venom with polished, polite, and calm tones. Then they smile. Consider the ways James described destructive words in verses 1-8.

Destructive words are like fire. They burn and destroy. You can't reverse the damage they do. A fire starts in one room, but it consumes the whole house. James described the effects as impacting the whole course of life. The idea is that of a wheel or a circle of physical effects, a series of events involving repeated patterns.

Words impact all of life. Consider how our words can consume (or feed) our children, other family members, church people, those we work with, and people we encounter casually.

Our habits with words can prompt any of these people to also use consuming (or nourishing) words. The fire spreads.

Destructive words are like poison. Poison brings death, similar to a venomous snakebite. Some people choose a bite that is just as venomous. It doesn't kill physically, but it brings death to a person's dream, hope, joy, peace, confidence, love, or desire.

Destructive words are like curses. When our words are restless and unruly, they are unstable. They can explode at any time. They can release a world of hurt.

> *How have you seen words act like fire or as poison?*
>
> **QUESTION #1**

> *"Kind words do not cost much. Yet they accomplish much."*
>
> —BLAISE PASCAL

James 3:9-12

It was a hot, humid day in the middle of Kansas City. The eight-hour shift seemed especially long for the veteran bus driver. Suddenly, a young woman, apparently upset about something, let loose with a string of unforgettable—and unrepeatable—words. Everyone around her was embarrassed by her string of profanity. Still mumbling, the angry passenger disembarked a few blocks later. As she stepped down, the bus driver calmly said, "Madam, I believe you are leaving something behind." She turned and snapped, "Oh, and what is that?" He replied, "A very bad impression."

We tend to limit the misuse of words to cursing, but it can include a wide variety of behaviors. For example, friends played a trick on Megan when she was 13 years old. These friends fabricated a boyfriend for Megan, named Josh, who struck up a cyber relationship with her. He had reportedly just moved to town and the conversation went well for six weeks. But then the imaginary Josh broke up with Megan, telling her she was fat, cruel, and not a good friend. Megan took her own life. Sadly, this was not just a teenage prank. At least one adult was also involved.

Words have power to destroy or to heal, to crush dreams or to feed them. Each word matters, whether we want it to matter or not. Our speech can be so inconsistent.

Destructive words defile us; they stain and ruin everything about us. No matter how we act, our speech can ruin it all. Words can ruin a reputation and void our Christian witness. Venting with anger may make you feel better for a brief moment, but it makes you look worse. It hurts and betrays others. And once words are out, you can't take them back. Destructive words are inconsistent with the indwelling Christ.

James 3:13-18

So how do we dodge the pressure of letting our mouths run amuck? We can't do it on our own. We need the power and wisdom of God in our lives. Consider these principles in light of what James 3:13-18 says:

▶ **Recognize when your speech is not right … and repent.** Reread 3:5 and read verses 13-18. Invite God to show you what your words actually create, not what you mean or don't mean for them to create. Then weed out any bitter envy, selfish ambition, evil, favoritism, disorder, and hypocrisy. Sow words that understand, are pure, build peace, nurture good fruits and are gentle, loving, and full of mercy. Look particularly at your humor.

▶ **Invite God to clean your heart.** The mouth speaks out of the overflow of the heart. So we all need heart surgery: the work of God purifying and changing you. See Psalm 51.

▶ **Transfer control to the Holy Spirit.** James 3:8 doesn't say the tongue cannot be tamed. It says no person can tame it. God, however, can do this through His Spirit. So transfer control of your tongue to God. Each time you speak, let Him filter and adapt your words. Without permission He will not control a lying, blaspheming, slanderous, or gossiping tongue. Nor will He deliver the drunk from alcohol, the gambler from the table, the addict from drugs, or the lustful person from adultery. Yet, I have witnessed in the lives of many converts that it is easier to forsake these behaviors than to get victory over a wicked tongue. The horse doesn't put a bit in its own mouth. The rider inserts the bit and controls the whole horse. The rudder drives the ship, but the captain controls the rudder. When we invite the Spirit of God to control us, our speech reflects that control.

> *How do our words define who we are?*

QUESTION **#3**

▶ **Determine to speak wisely.** Reread verses 13 and 17. Ask yourself before you speak:

Will my words give grace? "The words from the mouth of a wise man are gracious" (Ecc. 10:12a).

Will my words bring healing? "The tongue of the wise brings healing" (Prov. 12:18b).

Will my words promote life? "Life and death are in the power of the tongue" (Prov. 18:21a).

WHAT DO YOU SAY?

She asks you, "Does this outfit look good on me?" It doesn't.	
An incompetent co-worker calls you down in a meeting.	

> *When has your life been changed by wise and gentle words?*
>
> QUESTION #4

LIVE IT OUT

Here are three ways to choose and use only words filled with wisdom and gentleness:

▶ **Pray before you open your mouth.** Put James 3:13-18 into practice. Seek God's wisdom in what to say and how to say it.

▶ **For a week, keep a log of family conversations.** Were your words more a "blessing" or a "curse?"

▶ **Apologize.** If your words have gotten you into trouble, contact the person and use a different set of words: an apology.

Your words have power to nourish or to destroy. **It's your choice. Choose to keep your mouth out of trouble.**

Fuggeddaboudditt

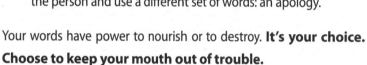

"ARE YOU IN THE MAFIA? All Eye-Talians are in the Mafia, aren't they?" For one of the rare times in my life, I was speechless and I wondered, Is this woman seriously asking me, "When you're not being a Christian speaker, do you and 'Uncle Tony' throw people wearing cement shoes in the East River?" Yes, I replied in my best guest-speaker voice, "Everyone in my family is a Christian. I don't know anyone in the Mafia."

To continue reading "Fuggeddabouditt" from *More Living* magazine, visit *BibleStudiesforLife.com/articles.*

My group's prayer requests

....

....

....

....

....

....

....

....

....

....

My thoughts

SESSION 5

THE PRESSURE OF CONFLICT

What conflicts and competitions do you find compelling?

Overcome the pressure of conflict by humbly submitting to Christ.

THE BIBLE MEETS LIFE

Franklin Roosevelt once said, "There is nothing I love as much as a good fight." Fighting comes naturally to many people. On any given day they'd rather go for the jugular than give in.

James wrote that we often find ourselves in the midst of fights, arguments, quarrels, or some kind of dispute. We feel the pressure to fight each other over politics, relationships, work, and church. We quarrel over money, religion, sports, you name it.

We even fight ourselves. We feel pressure caused by a lack of contentment and a restlessness in our spirits that can't seem to be satisfied.

We even feel pressure to fight God. You may be in conflict with God right now, stubbornly refusing to yield, foolishly holding on tightly to the lesser things of this world. James teaches us how to handle the pressure of conflicts so they don't become quarrels or wars.

WHAT DOES THE BIBLE SAY?

James 4:1-10 *(HCSB)*

1 What is the source of wars and fights among you? Don't they come from the cravings that are at war within you?

2 You desire and do not have. You murder and covet and cannot obtain. You fight and war. You do not have because you do not ask.

3 You ask and don't receive because you ask with wrong motives, so that you may spend it on your evil desires.

4 Adulteresses! Don't you know that friendship with the world is hostility toward God? So whoever wants to be the world's friend becomes God's enemy.

5 Or do you think it's without reason the Scripture says that the Spirit who lives in us yearns jealously?

6 But He gives greater grace. Therefore He says: God resists the proud, but gives grace to the humble.

7 Therefore, submit to God. But resist the Devil, and he will flee from you.

8 Draw near to God, and He will draw near to you. Cleanse your hands, sinners, and purify your hearts, double-minded people!

9 Be miserable and mourn and weep. Your laughter must change to mourning and your joy to sorrow.

10 Humble yourselves before the Lord, and He will exalt you.

Key Words

Adulteresses (v. 4) – In spiritual adultery, people choose substitutes over God.

the proud (v. 6) – The term refers to those who align their hearts with anyone or anything other than God, thus making Him their rival.

humble (v. 6) – The term conveys an attitude of lowliness, poverty, lack of power. Humble people have the right view of God and themselves. Rather than align themselves against God they learn from Him, trusting His leadership and will.

James 4:1-5

James began chapter 4 with a question. Where do our conflicts come from? If you are going to stop a fight, the best way to do it is to stop it at its source. James noted three sources of conflict:

▶ **Self-centeredness.** The lusts and pleasures in verse 1 come from the Greek word from which we get our word "hedonism." Our fleshly bodies long for pleasure—sexual or otherwise—and a life of ease. The pleasures of this world try to choke out God's Word in your life (Luke 8:14). They act like soldiers waging war against our soul (1 Pet. 2:11). Self-centered desire for pleasure makes us demanding, unfaithful, greedy, possessive, murderous, covetous, and envious.

▶ **Prayerlessness.** We fight because we don't have, and we don't have because we don't ask. Too often, we are so busy fighting that we don't have time to pray. Or we pray for the wrong things (v. 3). God is the giver of every good and perfect gift (Jas. 1:17). But we never know God's provision because we don't take time to pray. When we do pray, James says we don't always get because we ask from a bad place. Actually from a cruel, evil, sick place. We give our wish list to God with one aim in mind: satisfaction of our own evil and selfish desires. James says that wastes (that's what the word "spend" means in v. 3) God's blessing.

> *What cravings most often lead you into conflict?*
>
> QUESTION #1

▶ **Worldliness.** Verses 4-5 refer to embracing the world's values, living for the here and now, and seeking the world's treasures, glory, and recognition. Seeking the things of the world brings us into conflict with God. When you long for the things of this world, you commit adultery against God. Believers are the bride of Christ, and to turn from Him is unfaithfulness. Seeking the world also shows hostility toward God; we act hatefully and in opposition to Him, similar to before we knew Jesus (Rom. 8:7, Col. 1:21). To make God your enemy literally means to stand against Him.

CHECK YOUR MOTIVES

PRAYING FOR	SELFISH MOTIVE	CHRIST-CENTERED MOTIVE
Praying for more money		
Praying for a car		
Praying for someone's salvation		

How do motives relate to conflict?

QUESTION #2

James 4:6-10

James offers five practical ways to overcome the pressure of conflict:

1. Humble yourself. God is opposed to the proud. When we persist with arrogant, self-centered, self-seeking actions, then conflict and fights remain part of our experience. The pain of conflict is great, but James promises that God's grace is greater. And His grace—His help, favor, and blessing—are given to those who choose to be humble. Humble people are teachable. Humble people don't demand their way. Humble people admit their needs to God and others. Humble people don't seek the things of the world to validate them. Humble people find grace from God to start over and receive new strength. When you humble yourself in the presence of God, He will exalt you.

2. Submit to God. Submission is a command (v. 7). The verb "submit" is a compound word in Greek that means to align yourself under something or someone. Think of an organizational chart or a military formation. Christ is the head and we align ourselves under Him. Christ is our commander and we carry out His orders. We avoid and resolve conflict by laying down our rights and following Jesus.

3. Resist the Devil. The word "devil" in verse 7 is the Greek word *diablos*. It's where we get our word "diabolical." It's a compound word that means "to throw or hurl against." Satan casts insults and accusations against you. He whispers: "Demand your way," "Give them a piece of your mind," "You deserve better," "You can't let them get away with that," and many other lies and temptations. But the diabolical one only steals, kills, and destroys (John 10:10). So, stand against him. Take every thought captive to Christ (2 Cor. 10:5). Put on the armor of God (Eph. 6:10-17). Hide God's Word in your heart (Luke 4:1-12). My wife and I have learned that when our tempers burn hottest and we are really going at it, the only one winning is Satan. We've learned to stop and acknowledge that. My spouse is not the enemy; Satan is. We call that out for what it is: spiritual warfare. And then we work together to reject his attempt to devour our marriage.

> **What is involved in resisting the Devil?**
>
> **QUESTION #3**

When you resist the devil in the name of Jesus, he will flee. Why? Because you surrender to God and hide yourself in Him—Satan wants none of Jesus. That battle is already won.

4. Draw near to God. The Bible offers several ways to foster close fellowship with God:

▶ Read the Bible. It is God's love letter to you. It shows how to draw near to God's heart and plan.

▶ Listen to God. God welcomes and enjoys your conversation. Like any relationship, both listening and talking are a must. Bible reading is how God talks to you. Set a daily time to read and pray. Doing so will re-adjust the altitude and attitude of your heart, and shed the selfishness and worldliness that so often lead to conflict.

▶ Worship. Whether worshipping with your church family on Sunday or focusing on God during the week, keep God in your mind. When you draw near to God, He draws near to you.

5. Get rid of your sins. James commands us to cleanse our hands and purify our hearts. For conflict to end, we must own our faults and wrongs, and seek to be made right. Invite the Holy Spirit to take over. He aligns your hands and heart with God, the essence of holiness. Cleanse your hands through repentance. Purify your heart by letting Him make your heart holy. The word "purify" translates to the Greek word "holy." James adds that we need to purify our hearts because we are double-minded. More accurately, we can be double-souled. Our flesh and Satan appeal to our soul to turn from God. But the Spirit of God within us beckons us to yield to God and follow after Christ. The most miserable person in the world is the one who claims Christ, yet follows the flesh. We are not to have a divided soul.

> *What helps you draw near to Christ and humble yourself before Him?*

QUESTION #4

"In every encounter we either give life or we drain it. There is no neutral exchange."

—BRENNAN MANNING

LIVE IT OUT

When the pressure of conflict begins to rise in your life, take action. Based on the principles in James 4:1-10, consider these steps:

▶ **Check your motives.** Evaluate your desires to determine if they are self-centered or Christ-centered.

▶ **Submit to Christ.** Give up every thought and desire to the lordship of Christ.

▶ **Keep a prayer journal.** Keep the proper focus by identifying how each request can specifically honor Jesus.

Conflict may be compelling in the sports arena, but not in your life. **Quit competing with God and live humbly under Jesus Christ.**

Start Here

David felt like he was all alone—with a story no one in our small group could understand.

"Brittany cut her wrists last weekend. I don't believe she intended to take her life, but I definitely heard the cry for help," he said. "When I asked her why, she said, 'It isn't like you would miss me, Dad. You've always been so busy with your career. I've felt for a long time that I'm invisible to you.'"

To continue reading "Start Here" from *More Living* magazine, visit *BibleStudiesforLife.com/articles*.

My group's prayer requests

....

....

....

....

....

....

....

....

....

....

My thoughts

SESSION 6

THE PRESSURE OF RETALIATION

What makes you want to get even?

> *When someone wrongs you, respond with patient endurance.*

THE BIBLE MEETS LIFE

At age 73, Carl Ericsson was sentenced to life in prison. He's going to spend the rest of his life in jail because he decided to exact revenge on a former high school classmate who did him wrong. Ericsson found out where his old classmate lived, rang the man's doorbell, asked him his name, and then shot him to death. What prompted the shooting? The startling answer apparently was a 1950s locker room humiliation that festered in Ericsson's mind for a half-century.

How do you respond when you are humiliated? What do you do when you get cheated by a salesman or business associate? How do you handle it when your spouse lies or otherwise takes advantage of your trust? What do you do when you're wronged in another way?

James wrote to first century Christians who knew first-hand the pain of mistreatment and the pressure to exact revenge.

WHAT DOES THE BIBLE SAY?

James 5:1-11 *(HCSB)*

1 Come now, you rich people! Weep and wail over the miseries that are coming on you.

2 Your wealth is ruined and your clothes are moth-eaten.

3 Your silver and gold are corroded, and their corrosion will be a witness against you and will eat your flesh like fire. You stored up treasure in the last days!

4 Look! The pay that you withheld from the workers who reaped your fields cries out, and the outcry of the harvesters has reached the ears of the Lord of Hosts.

5 You have lived luxuriously on the land and have indulged yourselves. You have fattened your hearts for the day of slaughter.

6 You have condemned—you have murdered—the righteous man; he does not resist you.

7 Therefore, brothers, be patient until the Lord's coming. See how the farmer waits for the precious fruit of the earth and is patient with it until it receives the early and the late rains.

8 You also must be patient. Strengthen your hearts, because the Lord's coming is near.

9 Brothers, do not complain about one another, so that you will not be judged. Look, the judge stands at the door!

10 Brothers, take the prophets who spoke in the Lord's name as an example of suffering and patience.

11 See, we count as blessed those who have endured. You have heard of Job's endurance and have seen the outcome from the Lord. The Lord is very compassionate and merciful.

Key Words

patient (v. 7) – The Greek word is *makrothymeo*—makro- means long, and -thymeo means heat. It literally means long tempered. It carries the idea of waiting while depending on God.

blessed (v. 11) – The Greek word describes the happiness a believer can experience even while suffering.

endured (v. 11) – This means to have withstood with courage, especially under pressure.

James 5:1-6

Why shouldn't we get revenge? The simple answer is that it doesn't work. Among other failures, revenge just perpetuates the cycle of hurt and hate. The effective response is not to cave in to the pressure to retaliate, but instead to yield to God's leadership.

What are supernatural responses to being wronged? They all start with the assumption that God is better at repaying than we are. He knows what will work, when it will work, and what changes a heart.

While we wait for God to act, we don't just wait. We also follow God's instructions for what to do about the wrong. One of these instructions is to not treat others so they want to retaliate against us. James 5:1-6 describes some wealthy ones who had apparently lined their pockets through mistreatment of others. Becoming wealthy is not bad. Becoming wealthy by mistreating others is very bad. James sounded clear warnings to these cruel ones: your miseries are coming (v. 1); your wealth will rot and witness against you (vv. 2-3); the outcry of those you have mistreated has reached the Lord (v. 4); you have lived self-indulgently on the way to death (v. 5); and you have murdered righteous people (v. 6).

> *What emotion do you feel when you read James' words to the rich?*
>
> **QUESTION #1**

When you leave retaliation in God's hands:

▶ **You end the cycle of violence (Prov. 25:21-22).** Joseph was wronged by his brothers. Years later he could have killed them. But he chose to forgive and work to restore his family.

▶ **You express faith that God will be just (Rom. 12:17-19).** These verses say to not repay evil for evil and instead to do what is honorable.

▶ **You follow the example of Jesus (1 Pet. 2:21-24).** Jesus was reviled. He suffered. He has left us His example. We can follow in His steps.

James 5:7-8a

Having suffered incredible injustice, first-century Christians certainly felt the pressure to retaliate and to take their own revenge. Instead, James offered two better solutions to revenge: (1) choose patience and (2) strengthen your hearts.

The word "patient" in Greek is a compound word, combining the word "long" (*makro*) and "anger" (*thumos*). Patience is choosing to keep your cool and take a long time before you blow your lid. Patience is the choice to endure and bear suffering without staying angry.

You may be thinking patience isn't your spiritual gift; and that's true. Patience isn't a spiritual gift exercised by a few; it is the fruit of the Spirit to be demonstrated by all Christians (Gal. 5:22). Patience is a choice, not a feeling. Patience is evidence of God's love inside of us (1 Cor. 13:4). Choosing patience strengthens our hearts (Jas. 5:8).

Why choose patience? God can do a better job of repaying than you can. A day is coming when God will make all the wrong things right. When Jesus comes, His power and glory will be revealed, and He will overthrow every enemy. In that day, the wicked will be judged and our faithfulness will be rewarded.

God's justice may take time. But like a farmer waiting on the early and late rain, you trust that in due season, God will make all things right.

> *How can we work for justice without veering into retaliation?*

QUESTION #2

James 5:8b-11

Patience doesn't mean passivity. You don't just sit back and do nothing. James gives us three positive practices to perform while being patient.

1. **Strengthen your heart.** Verse 8 calls us to shore up, prop up, or tie down our hearts. The concept is that you make your heart immovable in the storms of life; you drop the anchor of your heart firmly into the character of God and Word of God. In 1 Samuel 30, the Amalekites raided David's city, burned his city, kidnapped his family, and kidnapped the families of David's men. David's own men, bitter about the loss of their sons and daughters, thought of stoning him. David was in great distress. But David strengthened himself in the Lord his God (30:6). That's what James tells us to do. You don't win spiritual wars with the weapons of your flesh. You win by waiting and trusting in God (Isa. 40:27-31). So if you are suffering and feel increasing pressure to lash out, resist. Be patient, call out to God, and ask for His strength.

2. **Stay positive in your attitude.** If complaining ever becomes an Olympic sport, some of us will win gold medals. But James says to quit moaning. Don't blame or begrudge others. Complaining is simply a forerunner for bitterness and hatred. When we get upset or hurt, our tendency is to take out our frustration on anyone who is near us. We snap at our family, fuss at our friends, or let loose with full-blown road rage on the commute home. James says don't complain against one another. When you complain against others, you put yourself in position to be judged. So do life without complaining or arguing (Phil. 2:14).

What does patience offer that retaliation or revenge never will?

QUESTION #3

3. **Stand with the prophets.** One way to bolster your resolve is to draw encouragement from those who have been there and done that. Think about people of faith like Elijah, Daniel, Jeremiah, Noah, Abraham, Moses, Ruth, Rahab, Esther, Sarah, and Job. Don't just stand with the old school prophets; lean also on present day people of faith. You'll find these people in your home, Bible study classes, accountability groups, and true Christian friendships. Encourage each other daily to stay in the fight and endure (Heb. 10:24-25).

RUMORS

A coworker circulates a rumor that costs you a significant promotion.

Responding with patient endurance will benefit me by:

Responding with patient endurance will benefit my coworker by:

Responding with patient endurance will benefit others by:

How do you lead someone to take his or her finger off the button of retaliation?

QUESTION #4

LIVE IT OUT

Carl Ericsson was sent to prison in 2012. But he had been in prison since the event first happened in the 1950s. Consider some ways you can live free:

- ▶ **Let it go.** If someone has wronged you, stop dwelling on it. Forgive and keep forgiving each time you remember the hurt.

- ▶ **Repay with kindness.** Find a specific way to do good to the one who has wronged you (See Rom. 12:17-21).

- ▶ **Work for justice.** Get involved with a Christ-centered organization that works on behalf of an oppressed group.

Instead of getting even, get free.

Nurture Not Neglect

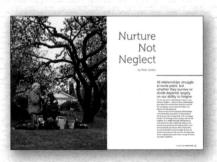

I've burned some relationship bridges in my lifetime. Bridges —plural. Some relationships may indeed be so toxic they must be severed. But sometimes those burned bridges show lack of forgiveness.

Most of us have a few ruptured relationships we've left behind. Recently, I've had a former friend on my mind. It's my fault we're no longer friends.

To continue reading "Nurture Not Neglect" from *More Living* magazine, visit *BibleStudiesforLife.com/articles*.

My group's prayer requests

....
....
....
....
....
....
....
....
....
....
....

My thoughts

Pressure Points

Over the last six weeks, as we've faced common pressure points seen in the Book of James, the ultimate goal has been for all of us to develop into people who know Christ and His gracious work, who are contributing servants in the community of faith, and who are effectively engaging the culture without losing distinction.

Christist

No one faced greater pressure than Jesus Christ, who faced incredible trials and temptations. However, Jesus endured the extreme trial and agony of the cross with joy, knowing what it would accomplish for us (Heb. 12:2). And because He never gave in to a single temptation, He was able to bring us forgiveness for our sins and empowerment to stand against temptation.

Community

Because anyone can become a part of the family of God, we are to treat all people with the same love we express to Christ. Consequently, when we stand together, we support and encourage each other in the midst of whatever pressures we are facing.

Culture

The body of Christ can truly impact the culture with their treatment of people who are different from them socio-economically, politically, and ethnically. A love for Christ that is expressed in love for all people can transform a society. The meekness and strong resolve of those who endure injustice patiently is a strong witness to the group or culture that oppresses them.

Society can be transformed by the quiet witness of those who endure opposition yet continue to love those who are against them.

LEADER GUIDE | PRESSURE POINTS

GENERAL INSTRUCTIONS

In order to make the most of this study and to ensure a richer group experience, it's recommended that all group participants read through the teaching and discussion content in full before each group meeting. As a leader, it is also a good idea for you to be familiar with this content and prepared to summarize it for your group members as you move through the material each week.

Each session of the Bible study is made up of three sections:

1. THE BIBLE MEETS LIFE.

An introduction to the theme of the session and its connection to everyday life, along with a brief overview of the primary Scripture text. This section also includes an icebreaker question or activity.

2. WHAT DOES THE BIBLE SAY?

This comprises the bulk of each session and includes the primary Scripture text along with explanations for key words and ideas within that text. This section also includes most of the content designed to produce and maintain discussion within the group.

3. LIVE IT OUT.

The final section focuses on application, using bulleted summary statements to answer the question, *So what?* As the leader, be prepared to challenge the group to apply what they learned during the discussion by transforming it into action throughout the week.

For group leaders, the *Pressure Points* Leader Guide contains several features and tools designed to help you lead participants through the material provided.

ICEBREAKER

These opening questions and/or activities are designed to help participants transition into the study and begin engaging the primary themes to be discussed. Be sure everyone has a chance to speak, but maintain a low-pressure environment.

DISCUSSION QUESTIONS

Each "What Does the Bible Say?" section features at least four questions designed to spark discussion and interaction within your group. These questions encourage critical thinking, so be sure to allow a period of silence for participants to process the question and form an answer.

The *Pressure Points* Leader Guide also contains follow-up questions and optional activities that may be helpful to your group, if time permits.

DVD CONTENT

Each video features teaching from Chip Henderson on the primary themes found in the session. We recommend that you show this video in one of three places: (1) At the beginning of group time, (2) After the icebreaker, or (3) After a quick review and/or summary of "What Does the Bible Say?" A video summary is included as well. You may choose to use this summary as background preparation to help you guide the group.

The Leader Guide contains additional questions to help unpack the video and transition into the discussion. For a digital Leader Guide with commentary, see the "Leader Tools" folder on the DVD-ROM in your Leader Kit.

SESSION ONE: THE PRESSURE OF TRIALS

The Point: Joyful trust in God will see you through all trials.

The Passage: James 1:1-4

The Setting: James wrote what is considered the earliest letter in the New Testament. He wrote to Jewish believers, providing practical principles for living the Christian life. From the earliest days of the church, believers have experienced trials that tested their faith, but we can rejoice in the midst of those trials because of the growth and endurance God is working into our lives.

Icebreaker: What pressures squeeze the joy out of life?

> *Optional follow-up:* Which of these has had the greatest impact on your life up to now? How have you learned to deal with this struggle, if you have?

> *Optional activity:* Add another level of involvement to this icebreaker experience by helping group members construct a "stress ball" during the discussion. Provide participants with a balloon and direct them to stretch the latex by inflating the balloon, then allowing it to deflate. Show participants how to fill their balloons with sand (preferably using a funnel) and tie off the neck to make a squeezable ball.

> - *Materials needed:* 1 balloon for each participant, 2 or more funnels, a bag of play sand, a measuring bowl or other instrument used to pour the sand through the funnel.

Video Summary: Chip opens the video by reminding us that pressure is universal and has many forms. We can determine the biblical meaning of "testing" or "trials" by context. This particular use in James is intended to pull you toward God, not away from Him. Chip highlights three words in James, first: *Consider.* This means we should weigh the facts, not the feelings. Often testing is not pleasant but we can still be joyful knowing that there is a payoff in the end. God will allow pain for the purpose of making you like Jesus. Second: *Surrender.* You can choose to lay down your protests and have joy despite your circumstances. Third: *Trust.* These are tests of your faith; God is testing to approve, not to fail. He wants you not only to trust *in* Him but to trust Him.

WATCH THE DVD SEGMENT FOR SESSION 1, THEN USE THE FOLLOWING QUESTIONS AND DISCUSSION POINTS TO TRANSITION INTO THE STUDY.

- Chip uses examples of people who endure trials with joy because of the payoff at the end. Can you give other examples? How are these similar to what God is doing in the lives of Christians you know?

- Discuss the three terms that Chip highlighted from our Scripture passage: Consider, Surrender, and Trust. How do these work together to help us find joy in our trials?

WHAT DOES THE BIBLE SAY?

ASK FOR A VOLUNTEER TO READ ALOUD JAMES 1:1-4.

Response: What's your initial reaction to these verses?

- What questions do you have about the text?

- What new application do you hope to get from this passage?

TURN THE GROUP'S ATTENTION TO JAMES 1:1-2.

QUESTION 1: What keeps you from reacting with joy when the pressure of life feels overwhelming?

This question requires much introspection so make sure you allow time to process. You'll want to work past pat answers like "other people."

Optional follow-up: When have you felt joy in the middle of a difficult situation? Why?

QUESTION 2: What emotions did you feel during your most recent trial?

Some members may not feel comfortable expressing their emotions or even describing them. You might model an answer that is attainable for most group members from your own recent experiences.

Optional follow-up: How can we appropriately process our emotions in the middle of a trial?

MOVE TO JAMES 1:3.

QUESTION 3: During your most recent trial, how did you see God walking with you?

Often the first answer will set the tone for the group. Encourage the group to explore other options to answering the question.

CONCLUDE WITH JAMES 1:4.

QUESTION 4: How have you been encouraged by the endurance of others during trials?

Optional follow-up: In what ways do you currently need encouragement during a trial?

It's important that you give an opportunity for group members to request support and encouragement if they desire to do so, but make sure not to force anything. Use this question to open the door for people to express their needs, but feel free to move on toward the next question or application if nobody chooses to walk through that door.

Note: The following question does not appear in the group member book. Use it in your group discussion as time allows.

QUESTION 5: Who in your life is good at making lemonade out of sour circumstances? Consider sharing their story with the group if appropriate.

This question might also afford a good opportunity for you as the leader to edify someone in the group and encourage members to do likewise.

LIVE IT OUT

Invite group members to consider steps they can take to reclaim their lives from the pressure of trials. Point out three ways in which to do this from our lesson:

- **Choose a joyful attitude.** Evaluate how a joy-filled attitude could alleviate the pressure you feel from life.

- **Share your story.** Explain to someone how, during a previous trial, God strengthened you through the difficult time.

- **Help someone who is struggling.** Find someone who is going through difficulty. Be available to listen, encourage, and help them.

Challenge: When you encounter a trial or difficult situation this week, take a step back and contemplate what it would look like to actively trust God in that situation. Ask yourself: "What behaviors can I change right now because I believe that God is with me?"

Pray: Ask for prayer requests and ask group members to pray for the different requests as intercessors. As the leader, close the prayer time by being the last person to take your petitions and praises to God. Be sure to encourage group members in their trials and pray that they have the courage and strength to stand fast, having joy in their circumstances.

SESSION TWO: THE PRESSURE OF TEMPTATION

The Point: God won't tempt me, but He will provide a way to resist temptation.

The Passage: James 1:13-18

The Setting: After writing about how we should respond to the trials we face, James turned his attention to temptations. We all face trials and temptations, but temptations do not come from God. James concluded this section by pointing our attention to what does come from God. He is the giver of all good things.

Icebreaker: What food tempts you to say yes to just one more bite?

Optional follow-up: How have you successfully resisted those "one more bite" moments in the past?

Optional activity: Bring a decadent dessert to the group and allow people to sample if they choose. Use the questions below to explore your group's emotional reactions to temptation.

- What emotions did you experience when you first saw the food?
- What emotions or sensations did you experience as you ate it?
- What emotions did you experience afterward?

Video Summary: In this video Chip talks us through James 1:13-18, our primary text. He focuses his teaching on the reality that we all face temptation—James talks about *when* we are tempted, not *if*. But we don't have to give in. We can overcome. Chip also discusses how the way we face temptation has a great deal to do with how we see ourselves. God sees us as saints, holy, called out, set apart from sin. And when we begin to see ourselves the way He sees us, we can begin to win the fight.

WATCH THE DVD SEGMENT FOR SESSION 2, THEN USE THE FOLLOWING QUESTIONS AND DISCUSSION POINTS TO TRANSITION INTO THE STUDY.

- Spend a few minutes discussing identity and who God says we are versus how we sometimes see ourselves. Lead the group to examine how an accurate picture of our identity could put us in a better position to fight temptation.
- Chip explains that in the process of being tempted, Satan will attempt to replace God's truth with lies in our minds. Ask group members: What process do you go through to (1) recognize the lies when they come up, and (2) replace those lies with God's truth?

WHAT DOES THE BIBLE SAY?

ASK FOR A VOLUNTEER TO READ ALOUD JAMES 1:13-18.

Response: What's your initial reaction to these verses?

- What questions do you have about the text?
- What new application do you hope to get from this passage?

TURN THE GROUP'S ATTENTION TO JAMES 1:13.
QUESTION 1: If temptations promise good but never deliver, why do we so often say yes to them?

MOVE TO JAMES 1:14-15.
QUESTION 2: In what ways are we tempted to satisfy a God-given desire in a sinful way?

This question is personal in nature, but don't force group members to divulge their own failures. Allow the discussion to focus on "people" in general, unless participants voluntarily choose to share their experiences.

Optional follow-up: How can we tell when we're satisfying a God-given desire in a sinful way? What symptoms do we show?

Optional activity: Give out nutrition labels from a sugary cereal. Invite the group to search the labels to name comparisons to temptation.

CONCLUDE WITH JAMES 1:16-18.
QUESTION 3: What are some other gifts God has provided that could help you resist temptation?

QUESTION 4: How can you support and encourage someone struggling with temptation?

Optional activity: Encourage group members to practice discerning God's way of escape by jotting ideas on The Circumstance; The Escape activity in their group member book. Let volunteers choose one circumstance and identify a way of escape God might provide. Encourage several ways of escape for each; this demonstrates God's escapes are custom designed for us.

Note: The following question does not appear in the group member book. Use it in your group discussion as time allows.

QUESTION 5: In what ways can the support and encouragement you might give others help you when you need an escape from your own temptations?

LIVE IT OUT
Invite group members to consider three steps they can take to fight the pressure of temptation:

- **Think about the temptations you face.** Pray, asking God to help you recognize and carry out His strategy to overcome each.
- **Memorize Proverbs 4:25.** Practice it in moments of temptation.
- **Find a friend you can trust.** Ask him or her to hold you accountable as you face temptation.

Challenge: Encourage participants to consider other ways they can fight the influence of temptation in their lives this week. Consider going further and asking them to keep a journal and record how God provided a way for them to escape temptations throughout the week.

Pray: As you close the session, ask learners to thank God for His love and provision. Encourage them to privately confess when they've given in to temptation. Close the prayer time by asking God to help group members be alert to moments when temptation is baiting them. Pray that they take the way of escape He provides.

SESSION THREE: THE PRESSURE OF PARTIALITY

The Point: God does not play favorites and neither should I.

The Passage: James 2:1-13

The Setting: James instructed his readers to reject the practice of showing favoritism. By giving preferential treatment to the wealthy, believers were dishonoring the poor. James wrote that God honors the poor who love Him, and he offered Old Testament proof that to show favoritism based on wealth or status is sin.

Icebreaker: Who or what does society value most?

> *Optional Follow-up:* Who or what do we value most within the church?

The group will be tempted to give "the right answer" here. Be sure to encourage transparency.

> *Optional Activity:* Add a visual layer to this icebreaker experience by bringing in several contemporary magazines and/or catalogues. Ask participants to begin answering the above question by looking through the magazines and catalogues and cutting out images that represent what society values most.

> - *Note:* Consider finalizing this experience by directing group members to make a collage by attaching their selected images to a sheet of paper or poster board.
> - *Supplies:* Several magazines and/or catalogues (at least one per person), scissors, glue or tape (optional), paper or poster board (optional).

Video Summary: Chip begins this video with the story of a friend who was encouraged to be prejudiced in her hiring practices as a manager. Thankfully she stood firm and God blessed her with good work elsewhere. James saw people being true to human nature as well and judging others with biased human eyes. We compare. We compare the rich and the poor, the beautiful and the less attractive, etc. We should be comparing to Jesus, which indeed makes us all look like beggars. Partiality causes us to 1) Miss God's heart. God loves the poor, widows, orphans, the overlooked. David is a great example of how God looks on the inside, the heart. Will we honor God's heart and see with His eyes? Partiality also causes us to 2) Violate the royal law: love God and love your neighbor as yourself. All sin violates God's royal law but God instead says, "Show mercy. Love them all."

WATCH THE DVD SEGMENT FOR SESSION 3, THEN USE THE FOLLOWING QUESTIONS AND DISCUSSION POINTS TO TRANSITION INTO THE STUDY.

- Have you ever been in a situation similar to Chip's friend where you were encouraged to discriminate? How did you handle that?
- With whom do you find it most difficult to apply the royal law? Why?

WHAT DOES THE BIBLE SAY?

ASK FOR A VOLUNTEER TO READ ALOUD JAMES 2:1-13.

Response: What's your initial reaction to these verses?

- · What questions do you have about these verses
- · What new application do you hope to get from this passage?

TURN THE GROUP'S ATTENTION TO JAMES 2:1-4.
QUESTION 1: What kinds of experiences affect who we want to be around?

Help group members to see that often prejudice occurs due to our culture, our preferences, or even our family of origin. Jesus doesn't want us to use any of those as excuses, but we do need to recognize them.

> *Optional follow-up:* Have you ever felt discriminated against? How did that make you feel? Why?

Be sure to head off this turning into a gripe session or allowing prejudices to be vented. The idea is to help group members empathize with those who deal with this problem, perhaps often.

MOVE TO JAMES 2:5-7.
QUESTION 2: Why is the heart of God so close to those who are poor and excluded?

You might want to be prepared with biblical examples, especially from the ministry of Jesus, that show this to be true.

> *Optional follow-up:* When do you typically interact with those who are poor and excluded?

> *Optional follow-up:* What emotions do you experience when you interact with those who are poor and excluded?

> *Optional activity:* Consider organizing a missions trip or ministry project for your group to work alongside the poor and excluded either in your community or abroad. There is no better way to see the world through God's eyes than to get out of your comfort zone and minister as Jesus did. Enlist help from your pastor or a local non-profit organization.

CONCLUDE WITH JAMES 2:8-13.
QUESTION 3: What are examples of showing honor versus playing favorites?

> *Optional follow-up using Luke 18:9-14:* Jesus told this parable because of "some who were confident of their own righteousness and looked down on everyone else." How have you seen "goodness" used as an excuse to play favorites?

QUESTION 4: What's at stake when I play favorites?

Help the group move past the surface level and strive to see the times when they view others through a human lens rather than through God's eyes. If discrimination is a common occurrence in your community, be prepared to take baby steps rather than long strides to help group members get to where James is challenging us all to be. If you get silence, lead with an example to which most everyone can relate.

>*Optional follow-up:* What's at stake when we play favorites as a group? As a church?

>*Optional follow-up:* What steps can we take to avoid playing favorites as a group? As a church?

Note: The following question does not appear in the group member book. Use it in your group discussion as time allows.

QUESTION 5: Why do you think we often judge others by appearances? What do we use as a filter for that judgment?

The idea is to help group members be introspective and further explore the lens through which we often see people.

LIVE IT OUT

Invite group members to consider ways they can take back their lives from the pressure of partiality. Point out these three ideas in the study material:

- **Check your attitude.** When you treat someone with partiality, check the attitude of your heart. Confess it to God.

- **Demonstrate God's love.** Deliberately say a kind word, welcome someone to your table, or build someone up. Go out of your way to care.

- **Build a friendship.** Spend time with someone you wouldn't typically relate to.

Challenge: Consider going out into your community to watch and pray. You might choose a park bench or a train station, somewhere there are lots of people. Or ride the bus around your town and pray as you go. Ask God to give you His heart and help you see the people you meet through His eyes.

Pray: Ask for prayer requests and ask group members to pray for the different requests as intercessors. As the leader, close the prayer time by being the last person to take your petitions and praises to God. Encourage each member to beg God to change the hearts of the group, the church, and the community to ever broaden their love for others and to be ambassadors of reconciliation to a lost and dying world.

SESSION FOUR: THE PRESSURE OF WORDS

The Point: Fuel your words with wisdom and gentleness.

The Passage: James 3:1-18

The Setting: James addressed the great impact a believer's speech can have on others. Using several word pictures—controlling a horse, steering a ship, igniting a forest fire, and taming an animal—James shows the power behind the tongue. He calls us to a life of consistent speech. James also calls believers to seek the wisdom that only comes from God.

Icebreaker: When did your mouth get you into trouble?

Optional Activity: Help participants think about the words they say by directing them to spend five minutes in conversation without using the word *and*. Ask participants to discuss the questions below in pairs or small groups, but announce they are to give themselves a point whenever they say the word *and*. The person with the fewest points after five minutes is the winner. Use one of the following conversation questions (consider writing these on a whiteboard or large sheet of paper):

- What have you liked most about the weather this week?

- What do you like best about your favorite movies?

- How would you describe the rules of your favorite sport to someone who's never played?

Video Summary: Chip begins by reminding us that the Bible teaches the tongue carries death and life, blessing and curse. He tells the story of a friend who is a devout Christian, a fine family man, a servant in the church and community. But high school basketball games turn him into a different guy. He has not tamed the tongue. Today's Scripture says that is not okay. Chip teaches that James compares the tongue to three things: a fire, a poison, and a curse. He then goes on to give examples of each. Perhaps most disturbing is the role the tongue plays in infecting and affecting the next generation. Thankfully, though, your words can be tamed according to James. In order to do so, you must: Repent. Surrender. Speak words of wisdom. Examples of this new posture include saying things like: I was wrong. I'm sorry. Please forgive me. I love you.

WATCH THE DVD SEGMENT FOR SESSION 4, THEN USE THE FOLLOWING QUESTIONS AND DISCUSSION POINTS TO TRANSITION INTO THE STUDY.

- Share an example of when you have seen the tongue carry death or life, blessing or curse.

- What is the process Chip describes in taming the tongue? What do you find most difficult in this process?

WHAT DOES THE BIBLE SAY?

ASK FOR A VOLUNTEER TO READ ALOUD JAMES 3:1-18.

Response: What's your initial reaction to these verses?

- What questions do you have about the text?

- What new application do you hope to get from this passage?

TURN THE GROUP'S ATTENTION TO JAMES 3:1-8.
QUESTION 1: How have you seen words act like fire or as poison?

If group members have already had an opportunity to comment on the power of words to spread life or death, focus on the way that ill-spoken words can infect and spread to others.

Optional follow-up: What motivates people to use words in harmful ways?

Optional follow-up: What are some "acceptable" forms of negative speech prevalent in today's culture? In the church? (Illustration: sarcasm, cursing, crude jokes, etc.)

MOVE TO JAMES 3:9-12.
QUESTION 2: Why do we remember negative words more than positive words?

This question offers an opportunity to personalize and perhaps bring healing to someone in the group who has been affected by negative words. You can always encourage openness by being transparent yourself.

Optional follow-up: When have you seen something good get ruined because of harmful words?

CONCLUDE WITH JAMES 3:13-18.

QUESTION 3: How do our words define who we are?

It may be that some group members do not accept the premise. In this case, you might direct the question generally before moving closer to home. The next question will afford that opportunity.

QUESTION 4: When has your life been changed by wise and gentle words?

If you can give an example of someone in the group to begin, it will help to encourage more response as well as giving your group a win. It's good for the group to recognize the role they play in building up one another.

Note: The following question does not appear in the group member book. Use it in your group discussion as time allows.

QUESTION 5: You've probably heard an expression like: "Sticks and stones may break my bones, but words will never hurt me." How do you feel about this statement? What has been your experience with this viewpoint?

LIVE IT OUT

Invite group members to consider steps they can take to take back their lives from the pressure of words. Point out three ways to do this:

- **Pray before you open your mouth.** Put James 3:1-18 into practice. Seek God's wisdom in what to say and how to say it.

- **For a week, keep a log of family conversations.** Were your words more a "blessing" or a "curse"?

- **Apologize.** If your words have gotten you into trouble, contact the person and use a different set of words: an apology.

Challenge: Pick a day in the coming week and see if you can avoid saying anything negative for that entire 24-hour period. Be prepared to talk about your experiences at the next group meeting.

Pray: Ask for prayer requests and ask group members to pray for the different requests as intercessors. As the leader, close the prayer time by being the last person to take your petitions and praises to God. Encourage members to confess the sins of the tongue during this time and to ask God to transform their tongues into instruments of blessing instead.

SESSION FIVE: THE PRESSURE OF CONFLICT

The Point: Overcome the pressure of conflict by humbly submitting to Christ.

The Passage: James 4:1-10

The Setting: Even the early church experienced dissension within the body, and James identified the source of their conflicts and pointed to the need for humility before God.

Icebreaker: What conflicts and competitions do you find compelling?

Optional activity: Begin the discussion by showing one or more clips involving conflict from today's entertainment media. These clips could include anything from sporting events to dramatic dialogue in a Hollywood film. (Be sure to avoid any clips that involve inappropriate content.)

Video Summary: Chip teaches about the pressure of conflict, which is really pressure that comes in relationship. He tells the story of two good friends who went into business together. Now they don't even speak. Marriages once promising, now the couples are filing for divorce over irreconcilable differences. Siblings at a funeral who squabble over stuff. Churches in conflict over minutia. And the problem is this: every one of us wants our way. That's what wrong. My way versus your way causes conflict. Chip identifies three things that are the problem: self-centeredness, prayerlessness (we don't ask), and worldliness (lust of the eyes, lust of the flesh, and the pride of life). This is simply adultery against God. How do we resolve conflict then? We flip the script: Be Christ-centered. Be prayerful. Be faithful to God. Jesus really is the answer as simplistic and churchy as that may sound. He is the Prince of peace who gives to us the peace that passes all understanding.

WATCH THE DVD SEGMENT FOR SESSION 5, THEN USE THE FOLLOWING QUESTIONS AND DISCUSSION POINTS TO TRANSITION INTO THE STUDY.

- Tell of a time when you saw a promising relationship become a terrible conflict instead. What did you learn from someone else's experience?
- It is sometimes said that the best way to restore a relationship with someone is to begin praying for them. Have you found that to be true? Explain.

WHAT DOES THE BIBLE SAY?

ASK FOR A VOLUNTEER TO READ ALOUD JAMES 4:1-10.
Response: What's your initial reaction to these verses?

- What questions do you have about the text?
- What new application do you hope to get from this passage?

TURN THE GROUP'S ATTENTION TO JAMES 4:1-5.
QUESTION 1: What cravings most often lead you into conflict?

Most of us have an appetite for conflict because we are selfish individuals at heart. Help group members face that reality, even if they are not willing to be completely open with one another.

Optional follow-up: How does today's culture push our buttons in connection with those cravings?

QUESTION 2: How do motives relate to conflict?

Often we focus upon the behavior rather than the heart of the persons involved in the conflict. Relating a story of personal conflict and reflecting upon the motives behind it will help others do likewise.

Optional follow-up: How can we apply "checks and balances" to our motives and cravings?

CONCLUDE WITH JAMES 4:6-10.
QUESTION 3: What is involved in resisting the Devil?

Optional follow-up: What can we know about the Devil from God's Word?

In both of these questions, you will naturally be drawn to consider how the Devil opposes God's people. This may lead to a broader discussion about the reality of evil and a personal Devil.

QUESTION 4: What helps you draw near to Christ and humble yourself before Him?

While this question demands a personal answer that you can model for the group, there are certain spiritual disciplines which will likely be mentioned such as Bible study, reflection, journaling, prayer, and fasting.

Optional follow-up: How can we work to draw near to Christ as a group?

Note: The following question does not appear in the group member book. Use it in your group discussion as time allows.

QUESTION 5: Why do you think conflict comes so naturally to us?

LIVE IT OUT

Invite group members to consider steps they can take to take back their lives from the pressure of conflict. Point out three ways from the study material:

- **Check your motives.** Evaluate your desires to determine if they are self-centered or Christ-centered.
- **Submit to Christ.** Give up every thought and desire to the lordship of Christ.
- **Keep a prayer journal.** Keep the proper focus by identifying how each request can specifically honor Jesus.

Challenge: This would be a great week to present the gospel to your group. Believers will be reminded of the importance of sharing their faith and those who are still considering a relationship with Christ will have an opportunity to do so. Help may be found at *LifeWay.com/salvation*.

Pray: Ask for prayer requests and ask group members to pray for the different requests as intercessors. As the leader, close the prayer time by being the last person to take your petitions and praises to God. Encourage members to list those with whom they have unresolved conflict and then challenge them to go to that person either to offer an apology or to extend forgiveness.

SESSION SIX: THE PRESSURE OF RETALIATION

The Point: When someone wrongs you, respond with patient endurance.

The Passage: James 5:1-11

The Setting: In his closing words, James wrote specifically to the rich people among the believers, calling them from their greedy and corrupt behavior. He condemned their actions that oppressed others. James also wrote to those who were experiencing oppression. Using the illustration of a farmer and the example of Job, James calls all believers to live with patient endurance.

Icebreaker: What makes you want to get even?

Optional activity: Help your group members practice patient endurance in the midst of pain by directing them to hold an ice cube in their hands for as long as possible. Pass out an ice cube to each participant and challenge them to squeeze it in their hand as long as they can stand the cold. When everyone has finished, use the following questions to unpack the experience:

- What sensations or emotions did you experience while holding the ice cube?
- What techniques did you use to deal with the pain of holding the ice cube in order to keep from letting it go?

Supplies needed: An ice cube for each group member, paper towels to clean up

Video Summary: Chip begins with an illustration of men in the navy who oppressed a cook on the ship. He follows that up with examples of things from everyday life that cause us to seek vengeance, at least in our minds: being cut off in traffic, being done wrong in school, etc. It feels natural to want to retaliate. But that doesn't solve anything. It's not pleasing to God. God is not saying to be a doormat nor to ignore justice for others. What is the Christian response to being wronged? Trust in God's justice. He's the judge, not us. And He will do a better job of it than we will. Be patient. Chip teaches that *patient* is a compound word meaning "to take a long time for your thermometer to boil over." Be slow to anger, not repressing anger but living out the fruit of the Spirit instead. Like a farmer, wait on the rain from God. God rewards. Scriptural examples are Daniel and Joseph. When men did evil against them, God used it for good in their lives. So He does in ours.

WATCH THE DVD SEGMENT FOR SESSION 6, THEN USE THE FOLLOWING QUESTIONS AND DISCUSSION POINTS TO TRANSITION INTO THE STUDY.

- Share an example of when you retaliated on someone, but it didn't work out so well. How might it have gone better had you left it to God?
- When have you seen God's justice at work? How did that work out for the injured party? Feel free to use a biblical example.

WHAT DOES THE BIBLE SAY?

ASK FOR A VOLUNTEER TO READ ALOUD JAMES 5:1-11.
Response: What's your initial reaction to these verses?

- What questions do you have about the text?
- What new application do you hope to get from this passage?

TURN THE GROUP'S ATTENTION TO JAMES 5:1-6.
QUESTION 1: What emotions do you feel when you read James' words to the rich?

Optional follow-up: Who qualifies as "rich" in today's society?

Certainly these questions are not meant to foster political debate so be careful not to allow the conversation to be steered in that direction. Instead, help the group empathize with those who are being taken advantage of while understanding that James doesn't necessarily have salary numbers in mind here.

MOVE TO JAMES 5:7-8A.
QUESTION 2: How can we work for justice without veering into retaliation?

Optional follow-up using Romans 12:17-21: These verses command us to avoid revenge and instead wait for God's wrath to punish injustice and wrongdoing. How do we go about this kind of waiting?